WHALES

by Joan Short and Bettina Bird

Illustrated by Deborah Savin

This edition first published in the United States in 1997 by
MONDO Publishing
By arrangement with MULTIMEDIA INTERNATIONAL (UK) LTD

The publisher and authors would like to thank Sylvia M. James, Director of Education Programs, National Aquarium in Baltimore, Baltimore, Maryland; Professor Michael Bryden, University of Sydney, Australia; Mr. Robert Warneke, Department of Conservation Forests and Lands, Australia; and Dr. Stephen Whiteside, Project Jonah, Victoria, Australia, for their advice and assistance.

Photograph Credits: Fred Felleman/Tony Stone Images: front cover; © Ralph and Daphne Keller/A.N.T. Photo Library: p. 4; © Greenpeace: p. 5; © N.H.P.A./A.N.T. Photo Library: p. 6; Professor Michael Bryden: p. 7; Mike Osmond: pp. 12, 23; Stephen Whiteside: pp. 13, 28; Animals Animals/© Michael Sacca: p. 14 left; Peter Corkeron: pp. 14 right, 15; Paul Hodda: p. 16; William Rossiter: pp. 17, 19, 20; © Frank Todd: p. 24; R. J. Tomkins/A.N.T. Photo Library: p. 29.

Text copyright © 1988 by Joan Short and Bettina Bird
Illustrations copyright © 1988 by Multimedia International (UK) Ltd

For information contact:
MONDO Publishing
980 Avenue of the Americas
New York, NY 10018
Visit our web site at http://www.mondopub.com

Printed in Hong Kong
First Mondo Printing, October 1996
04 05 06 07 08   9 8
Originally published in Australia in 1988 by Horwitz Publications Pty Ltd
Original development by Robert Andersen & Associates and Snowball Educational
Designed by Deborah Savin   Cover redesign by Charlotte Staub

Library of Congress Cataloging-in-Publication Data
Short, Joan.
    Whales / by Joan Short and Bettina Bird ; illustrated by Deborah Savin.
      p.   cm. — (Mondo animals)
    Includes index.
    Summary: Discusses the physical features, social behavior, swimming and breathing techniques, communication, migration, and other facets of whales.
      ISBN 1-57255-190-9 (pbk. : alk. paper)
      1. Whales—Juvenile literature. [1. Whales.] I. Bird, Bettina. II. Savin, Deborah, ill. III. Title. IV. Series.
    QL737.C4S488   1996
    599.5—dc20   96-15298
                                                               CIP
                                                               AC

Cover: Killer Whale (Orca)

Contents

 # Introduction

Most people know that whales are large animals that live in the oceans. But not many people realize that dolphins and porpoises belong to the group of animals called whales, or *cetaceans.*

Whales — Mammals of the Sea

Although whales live in the oceans, they are not fish. Whales are mammals.

Mammals are animals that feed their young on milk. They also have lungs and breathe air, have a backbone, and are warm-blooded.

Mammals are called "warm-blooded" because their blood temperature does not go up and down when the temperature of their surroundings changes.

Right: A killer whale feeding

Opposite: An Indo-Pacific humpback dolphin. Like all whales, dolphins breathe air.

Physical Features

Body

All whales have two front fins, called *flippers*, and two strong, flat tail fins called *flukes*, which are joined together. Many species of whale also have another fin on their backs. This is called a *dorsal* fin.

Whales have smooth leathery skin. Under the skin is a thick layer of fat called *blubber*.

A Fin Whale

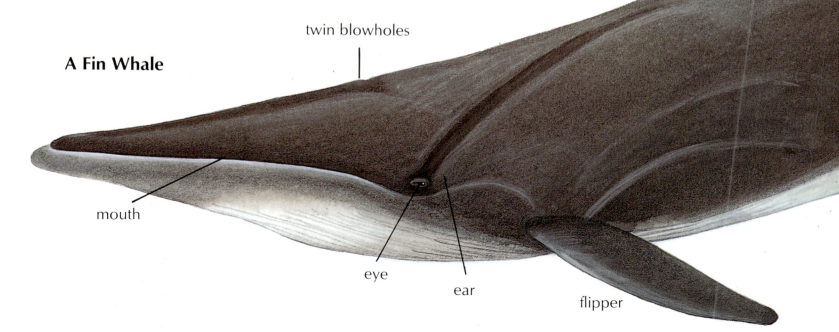

twin blowholes

mouth

eye

ear

flipper

Whales have two eyes, one on each side of the head, and they have two ears. The opening of each ear is a tiny hole, about the size of a pinhead, just behind the eyes.

Some species of whale have a single nostril, or *blowhole* on top of the head. Other species have twin blowholes.

Head of a Bottlenose Dolphin

single blowhole

dorsal fin

skin

fluke

Size

There are at least seventy-five species of whale, and they range in size from over 98 feet (30 meters) in length to less than 10 feet (3 meters).

Blue whales are the largest animals that have ever lived. They are even larger than any of the dinosaurs that once roamed the Earth. A blue whale may grow to over 98 feet (30 meters) in length and weigh more than twenty elephants.

One of the smallest whales is the common dolphin. It grows to a length of about 8 feet (2 ½ meters) and weighs about 180 pounds (82 kilograms).

killer whales
30 feet (9 meters)

humpback whale
56 feet (17 meters)

common dolphins
8 feet (2.4 meters)

grey whale
42 feet (15 meters)

sperm whale
60 feet (18 meters)

bowhead whale
65 feet (19.8 meters)

spectacled porpoise
7 feet (2.1 meters)

bottlenose dolphins
12 feet (3.8 meters)

southern right whale
56 feet (17 meters)

blue whale
98 feet (30 meters)

narwhal
16 feet (5 meters)

fin whale
88 feet (26.8 meters)

11

 # Swimming

When a whale swims it moves its powerful tail up and down, and beats the water with its flukes. Its flippers help the whale to steer and to keep its balance in the water.

A whale's streamlined body and smooth skin allow it to slip easily through the water.

Some whales *lobtail*. This means that they lift their flukes above the surface and slap them down hard on the water.

Breathing and Blowing

Whales must come to the surface of the water to breathe through their blowholes. However, most whales can hold their breath under water for about ten minutes or more, and sperm whales can stay under water for more than an hour.

When whales come to the surface they breathe out most of the air from their lungs. This air forms a mist called a *spout* or a *blow*.

After whales blow they breathe in fresh air and then dive again.

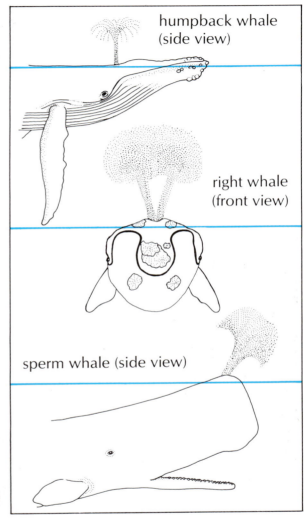

humpback whale (side view)

right whale (front view)

sperm whale (side view)

Above: Species of whale can sometimes be identified by the shape of their *spout* or *blow*.

Left: The twin blowholes of a right whale

The Two Groups of Whales

Right: An Indo-Pacific humpback dolphin. All dolphins have teeth in both the upper and lower jaws, and they usually have pointed or "beaked" heads.

Below: Dall's porpoise. One difference between porpoises and dolphins is that porpoises do not generally have beaked heads.

When scientists talk about whales they divide them into two groups — *toothed whales* and *baleen whales*.

Toothed Whales

All toothed whales have teeth. But the teeth of some species of toothed whale never break through the gums, and so the teeth are not seen.

All toothed whales have a single blowhole.

Feeding Habits

Toothed whales use their jaws and teeth to seize, hold, or bite their prey. Like all whales, they do not chew but swallow food whole.

All toothed whales eat fish but some eat other sea creatures as well. For example, sperm whales eat mainly giant squid, which live deep in the ocean. Sperm whales dive deeper than any other species of whale in their search for food.

Killer whales feed on fish, seals, walruses, and even other whales. They swallow small prey whole and bite pieces out of larger prey.

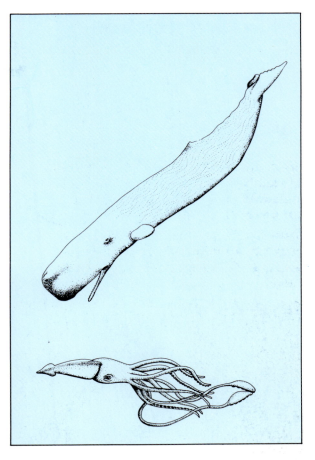

Above: A sperm whale catching a giant squid. Sperm whales have teeth only in the bottom jaw. When the mouth is closed, the teeth fit into sockets in the top jaw.

Left: A dolphin catching a fish. A dolphin swallows a fish head first so that the fish's fins fold back and do not stick in the dolphin's throat.

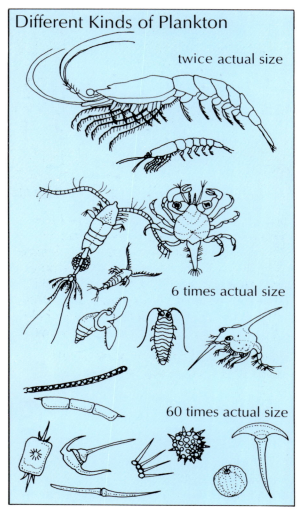

Different Kinds of Plankton

twice actual size

6 times actual size

60 times actual size

Above: Some examples of ocean plankton

Right: A close-up of the baleen of a Bryde's whale

Baleen Whales

Baleen whales do not have teeth. Instead, they have long fringes of bristly *whalebone* that hang down from the upper jaw, inside the mouth. The strands of whalebone are called *baleen*.

All baleen whales have double blowholes.

Feeding Habits

Baleen whales feed on ocean *plankton*. Plankton is the floating mass of very tiny creatures and plants that drifts in seas and lakes.

When a baleen whale is feeding it swims slowly with its mouth wide open. The whale's large mouth takes in both plankton and seawater. The seawater strains out and the plankton is trapped by the bristly baleen. The whale then closes its mouth and swallows the food.

Above: Some baleen whales, such as blue whales, have long grooves, like pleats, on the throat and chest. Such baleen whales are called *rorquals.* The "pleats" stretch widely when a rorqual is feeding and this allows it to take in an enormous amount of food with each mouthful. The throat of the blue whale in the photograph is full of food and water.

Left: The gaping jaws of a baleen whale taking in plankton and water

Social Behavior

Whales are known as *social* animals because they usually live in groups. These groups may be called *pods*, *herds*, or *schools*.

Some whales, such as blue whales, usually live in family groups that have a *bull*, one or two *cows*, and several *calves*.

Other whales move across the oceans in larger groups. Humpbacks do this and so do many dolphins. There may be twenty or more humpbacks in a herd, and hundreds or even thousands of dolphins in a large school or herd.

Whales help one another. When a mother sperm whale dives to catch squid other females in the herd protect her calf. And when a blue whale cow is sick or injured the bull will often stay with her.

Opposite: A pod of killer whales

Below: Dolphins will sometimes assist an injured companion. Two dolphins support the injured one so that its blowhole is above the surface of the water and it can breathe.

# Communication

Hearing

All whales have very good hearing and they communicate mainly by means of sound.

Whales can hear a range of sounds, from those that are very low-pitched to those that are very high-pitched. They can also tell from which direction under water a sound is coming.

Producing Sound

A baleen whale surfacing near boats

Whales can produce a variety of sounds. Scientists use underwater microphones, called hydrophones, to listen to sounds made by whales. Scientists have discovered that a whale makes distress calls if it is injured or in trouble, and that other whales may then come to its assistance.

Different species of whale make different sounds to communicate. Sperm whales make clicking sounds; bowhead whales make low moaning sounds; dolphins make whistling sounds. Humpback whales make patterns of sound, like music, and their "songs" may last for several hours.

 # Echolocation

Many species of toothed whale make special sounds that help them to locate objects in the water.

The sounds made by whales travel through the water as *sound waves.* When the sound waves hit an object in the water they bounce back as echoes, which the whales hear. This process is called *echolocation.* Echolocation helps the whales to move through water without bumping into obstacles such as rocks.

The sounds whales use for echolocation seem to be different from the sounds they use for communication. Dolphins make clicking sounds for echolocation and they can tell from the echoes where an object is, how large it is, and whether or not it is moving.

If it seems that something dangerous lies ahead, dolphins usually swim away from it. If there seems to be no danger, dolphins will often swim close to an object to find out more about it.

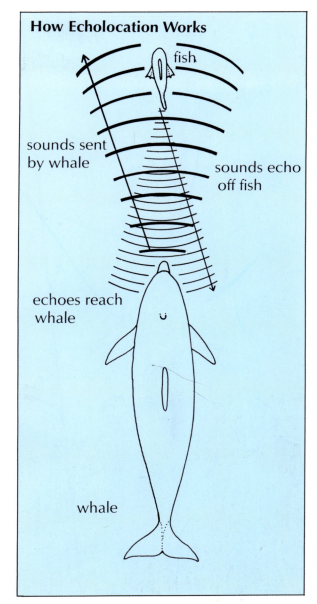

How Echolocation Works

fish

sounds sent by whale

sounds echo off fish

echoes reach whale

whale

Reproduction

In some species of whale a calf is born eight months after its parents have mated. In other species the calf is not ready to be born for several more months. Blue whale calves take eleven months; sperm whale calves take sixteen months.

Whale calves are born tail first, near the surface of the water. They must start swimming immediately, or they will sink, and they must breathe very soon after they are born, or they will drown.

A common dolphin giving birth to her calf

22

The mother may nudge the calf towards the surface to take its first breath of air. Other female whales may help.

Whale calves feed on their mothers' milk, but they do not have lips and they cannot suck. When a whale calf nuzzles one of its mother's milk glands, milk squirts into its mouth.

For at least a year calves swim close to their mothers, who will fight fiercely to protect them.

A humpback whale mother and her calf

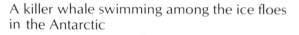

Migration

Some species of baleen whale live most of their lives in warm waters but other baleen whales *migrate* from the polar oceans to the tropics.

The migrating whales spend the summer months feeding in the cold polar oceans. In the icy-cold waters the whales' blubber prevents their body heat from escaping, and this stops them from getting too cold. But in most species the newly-born calves have very little blubber to keep them warm. So, when the polar summer is over, and before the

A killer whale swimming among the ice floes in the Antarctic

calves are born, the whales migrate to the warm tropical oceans. Here, the pregnant cows give birth to their calves.

There is very little plankton in tropical waters, so the migrating whales hardly feed there at all. They survive on the blubber stored under their skin and the new calves feed on their mothers' milk.

When the calves are strong enough, and have enough blubber, the migration back to the polar feeding grounds begins.

This map shows the feeding grounds and annual migration routes of herds of grey, fin and humpback whales.

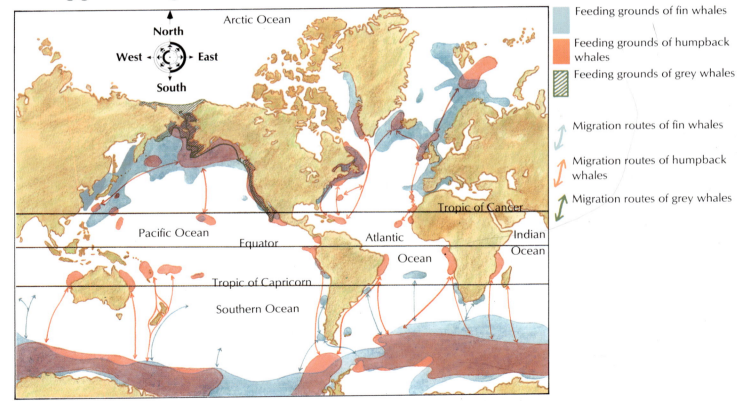

Feeding grounds of fin whales

Feeding grounds of humpback whales

Feeding grounds of grey whales

Migration routes of fin whales

Migration routes of humpback whales

Migration routes of grey whales

Arctic Ocean

North

West — East

South

Tropic of Cancer

Pacific Ocean

Equator

Atlantic

Ocean

Indian Ocean

Tropic of Capricorn

Southern Ocean

# Whale Hunting

For hundreds of years people have hunted whales for their blubber, whalebone, and meat. Oil from whale blubber was once used as a fuel for lamps. Whalebone—baleen—was used to stiffen corsets and to make the hoops for hooped skirts. Whale meat was eaten by people in some countries.

Early in the 1900s, factories began to use whale oil to make items such as margarine, cosmetics, and soap. Whalebone and whale meat were turned into fertilizer, or sold as pet food.

This etching, printed in the 1800s, shows
how whales used to be hunted.

Protection

It is estimated that between 1956 and 1966 about 574,000 whales were killed worldwide. So many whales were being killed that it seemed as if some kinds, such as right whales and blue whales, would become extinct. People began to urge governments to stop whaling. By 1982, only Norway, Russia and Japan were still hunting whales. Japan stopped whaling in 1988.

These days, we do not need whale oil; we use other oils. We do not need whalebone; we use plastics. And whale meat is eaten in very few countries. So we do not need to continue to kill whales. Whales should be protected by all countries so that no species becomes extinct.

Right: Sometimes whales become stranded on a beach where they usually die. These people are trying to help a whale to get back into the water.

Opposite: Bottlenose dolphins swimming in front of ship.

Glossary

breach	to break clear of water, usually head-first
bull	adult male (whale)
calf	young (whale)
cow	adult female (whale)
dorsal fin	fin on the back
extinct	no longer existing; having died out
floe	floating sheet of ice
migrate	to travel long distances; to come and go with the seasons
nuzzle	to prod or rub gently against (usually with the nose)
polar	at or near either of the Earth's poles; inside the Arctic or Antarctic Circles
prey	animal that is hunted or killed for food
sound wave	invisible "wave" that carries sound
species	group of animals (or plants) that cannot breed successfully with another group; group of animals (or plants) that have many features in common
tropical	between the Tropics of Cancer and Capricorn

Pronunciation Guide

cetacean	(se-*tay*-shun)
flukes	(flewks)
hydrophone	(*hy*-dra-fone)
migration	(my-*gray*-shun)
species	(*spee*-sheez)

Index

Note:
Page numbers in italic refer to illustrations.

31